# HOLD

# BOB HICOK

# HOLD

COPPER CANYON PRESS
PORT TOWNSEND, WASHINGTON

Cover art: James Ewing / OTTO, photograph of Ann Hamilton's
"The Event of a Thread," Park Avenue Armory, New York.

Copper Canyon Press is in residence at Fort Worden State Park in
Port Townsend, Washington, under the auspices of Centrum. Centrum
is a gathering place for artists and creative thinkers from around the
world, students of all ages and backgrounds, and audiences seeking
extraordinary cultural enrichment.

LIBRARY OF CONGRESS CATALOGING-IN-PUBLICATION DATA

Names: Hicok, Bob, 1960– author.
Title: Hold / Bob Hicok.
Description: Port Townsend, Washington :
Copper Canyon Press, [2018]
Identifiers: LCCN 2018021286 | ISBN 9781556595448
(pbk. : alk. paper)
Classification: LCC PS3558.I28 A6 2018 | DDC 811/.54—dc23
LC record available at https://lccn.loc.gov/2018021286

98765432 FIRST PRINTING

COPPER CANYON PRESS

Post Office Box 271
Port Townsend, Washington 98368
www.coppercanyonpress.org

FOR EVE

# CONTENTS

# HOLD

## The big book of therapy

If you think of humans as rare
as snowflakes, your world
is constantly melting.

If you think of humans as essential
to keeping dogs happy,
someone will always want
to buy you a beer.

## Flight plan

I like to think I have a wing
inside myself, and if a wing,
that I've swallowed Icarus whole,
wax and all, in the moment
before the sun treats him
as an equal. There's a poem about him
I love about a painting about him
I plan to stand before
before I die, flapping my arms
until the docent comes over
in his sturdy shoes and holds a mirror
so I can touch up my lipstick
before kissing the splash Icarus made
in the ocean going home. I have
all these plans to make plans
and all these desires to be brave
about the fall awaiting us all,
but I never quite get there,
like a man trying to leap
out of his tracks in snow. When
he lands, the first person
to welcome him back to earth
looks so much like the person
he tried to leave behind
that he leaps again, and spends
half of the rest of his life
landing, half in the air.

## Faith

Judaism would be more popular
without gefilte fish, I tell my wife's rabbi
every time I see her at the grocer's
getting her sustenance bagged
by the Holocaust denier
who lives down the street from me, a nice kid
who's a Nazi out of loneliness,
unlike his friend, who's a Nazi
out of tradition, his father telling me once
the same brand of shit I've heard my whole life
about Jews or blacks or people with elbows
other people don't like, with dance moves
and ideas that breed fire or need a shave,
and the cool thing about her is
she's working on the kid, on his big eyes
and spasmodic smile, by talking to him
about baseball and Auschwitz and girls
and girls and BMX bikes and Zyklon-B,
she talks to anyone who has a face,
who won the lottery of breath,
and she'll get there with him,
if not his pal, is my prediction
for evolution in my little burg, teeter teeter teeter
totter, something tips, something falls
in some minds and decency
wakes up, blood notices blood
and one day he'll realize
he doesn't even know what *kike* means,
and how alone he is,
and why punch the world in the face
when that's a very big face

and hands are fans of hold
more than shatter

## Bounty

Called my mother on Mother's Day.
Her shoulder hurt. Under her breast hurt.
Her back hurt where it had hurt
for fifty years. That's half a century of pain
thanks to evolution's idea that we should stop
running around on all fours and stand
against tyranny. She deserves a break
from realism, I thought. Realism informs us
the knees are the first to go
if you shoot someone in the knees.
I told her I was sending a painting
with actual leaves and peeing dogs in it.
It didn't matter it was a lie. The point of love
is to lie consistently and with an eye
toward the better world that will never exist.
Besides, at her age, she forgets who said what.
I'm sure she got off the phone, looked outside
and noticed she was surrounded by trees
and peeing dogs. The echo of what I'd said
felt like coming home after years
floating on an iceberg. The pains lessened,
if only briefly. I was a good son, if only briefly.
The question isn't when will her suffering end
but why do mothers only get one day a year
to make us struggle to figure out how to thank them?
That's think-tank shit, year-round shit.
That's deep shit, which leads eventually
to fields of wheat and fields of flowers.

## Up up and away

My brother and I quickly added up
what he'll need to retire. He was calling from work,
on a break, and worrying how expensive it is
to get to the finish line, let alone die.
He wouldn't want me to tell you the figure,
but we're friends and you never say much
anyway, so here it is—a shit ton. There's
the British shit ton, or shite tonne. The Scheiße Tonne
and the mierda tonelada. Linguists will tell you
to pass the scungilli and that the shit ton exists
in every language. So. What we concluded is
my brother needs a raise, or to start robbing banks
or people who rob banks or stagecoaches,
being traditionalists. I tried to cheer my brother up
by reminding him all clowns die too, some
in gruesome tuxedos, others in bed
reading *Clown Monthly: A Journal of Smiles.* He laughed,
but under the laugh I could hear a rock crusher
going to work. It says a lot that in this life,
even rocks get beat up. This is when I want the Marines
to parachute in and save the day or at least
two o'clock. But do I get my way? No. Do you? Hell no.
Does anyone? I'd like to meet someone who gets her way
and ask what that's like, having your cake
and strumming your banjo too. A man can dream.
The good news is that means he's sleeping and safe.
The bad news is predictable: Ice Climber Falls
Into the Sun. If I had a nickel for every time
I wonder why the expression isn't,
If I had a million bucks for every time
I wished I had a million bucks,
I'd own the Pacific Ocean and change its name

to Ruth. This is not the life we wanted, is it?
Maybe we get another chance. Maybe
there'll be an ice sculpture of a swan
at the next party and I'll smile
at the coldness of beauty and finally
be assuaged by aesthetics and the right amount
of champagne. No, not a shit ton
or sip ton or any kind of ton. Two glasses
does it for me. Two glasses
and I believe things are looking up
when I'm counting stars, three thousand
and eleven, so far.

## Objectivity

Now that cellphones
come with a conscience,

we know that the moment
he gave in, the second the wind

left his body and he accepted
the orthodoxy of your cop

fist, was nineteen punches
before you quit. Besides

your smile, another fact
the video makes clear:

equality means either
you stop beating

black jaywalkers or start
beating me.

# Eve

Though I am not her stethoscope,
she sanctions the wanderings of my ears
across her body, my listening to the light sanding of wood
that is her breathing, to her closed eye still warm
from touching the moon. And down there, where she turns
into a Y, it's fun to whisper into her cave and listen for the echo
coming back changed. As when I said, *My shadow
is a critique of my heart*, her vagina replied, *You try too hard
to prove you exist*, the best game of telephone I've ever played,
with any woman, let alone a woman named
for the first woman to run and run until she realized
she could never be lost because maps didn't exist. And if they did,
she'd have made them, and if she had made them,
they'd have been maps of water, to water, by water, for water
to get back to where water began, every one of them
left out in the rain.

## Poem ending with a murder/suicide

It's interesting to me there's a minimum
but no maximum wage. One without the other
seems like pants without legs or love
without someone to love. So what
are the groups—people
who want no minimum or maximum wage;
people who want a minimum
but no maximum wage; people
who want a minimum
and maximum wage; and people
who want to eat. A minimum wage
of twenty bucks an hour
is roughly eight hundred a week,
or forty grand a year,
or 1.6 million in a life. There's
your maximum wage—1.6 million a year.
If you earn in a year
what I earn my entire life,
you deserve the right
to be happy about it
in a gated community
where you don't have to be ashamed
of the dance of your joy.
I deserve the right
to put heirloom tomatoes
in the salad now and then.
Such as when my kid
got her cast off
and her hand looked fine,
like it intended to go on waving
at moonlight and birds.
And I never thought about it

but slipped the insurance card
out of my wallet and slid it over.
And the car started
the first time
for the drive home
to our little bungalow
that needs a new paint job
but that'll happen this summer,
right before we go to a lake
for a few days and I open a beer
one night and think, I have a place
in whatever this is.
Then listen to the stars
saying nothing in peace
or what passes for peace
is a mystery to me,
not unlike who's behind
the universe or why so many people
in unions voted for people
who wanted to kill unions, but we did
and they died, unions died.
Now where on Earth
am I supposed to send the flowers?

## The South is the country I live in now

How I got talking to the guy I don't remember
on Sullivan's Island. Our dog was still alive
and had walked repeatedly illegally
on the beach according to the signs. Dolphins
needled back and forth, stitching waves together
almost close enough for me to hit them
with a rock, had I a better arm and more spite.
My wife held the shell of her sea-sounding head
to the shell of mine, we were empty
of worry and work and had seen where turtles
had come in to lay their eggs, I think
is what I pointed out to the guy
casting his line into an ocean to ask
what bounty it cared to share. Or the existence
of weather. Surrealism in French cooking. Whatever
we were talking about, smack-dab in the middle
or muddle of a sentence, I realized
I was looking at Fort Sumter and said, *Oh my God,
that's where the Civil War began,* my God
being no god but who's counting. And without
changing expression or clothes, levity or levitation,
he said, *Yes, that's where the War
of Northern Aggression began.* You should probably
know we were standing where slaves
had been brought in, since that's still a thorn
or red-hot poker in the paw of America
we're aces at pretending isn't there. Our height,
weight, color were very similar, and yet, had I or he
a womb or even eight, there's not a chance
we'd ever procreate, based solely on our views
of an island, making us technically
different species. I'm only thinking that

now. In the moment, what stood out was the gap
between the end of my sentence and the beginning
of his, something like a thousandth
of a breath, meaning the idea that the South
and slavery should have been left alone
is a loaded gun he carries everywhere he goes.
And of course we're not different species
but two guys with the same number of legs
and heads and chromosomes, sons of the same mother
fucking war that isn't over.

## Verve is to élan what kissing is to kissing longer

Unto my soul, I wear a crown of Legos
you can't see.
I am the king of doing wheelies
on the Sting-Ray bicycle of my mind
while breaking rocks beside you
and every other convict
in sales. Sure, what kind of royalty
burps root beer out his nose?
I understand how far I am
from the example Darth Vader set
by blowing up planets
to teach the universe who's boss.
Light is boss, which makes god
Employee of the Month
every month. Every second,
a little less than a second passes
if I go fast enough downhill,
so technically I'm always
in bonus time. What's that old saying—
you have to break a lot of eggs
against your forehead to make
the most stubborn child laugh.
I'm taking the tree swing at face value
as the only currency
the afterworld will accept
and holding on to my *yippees*
until they're vintage or classic
or whatever the hip nomenclature is
among the avant-gardians,
the guys and gals who are part of team
Black Hole. I'm part of team
Yes You Can Divide by Zero. It's messy,

but so are the best burritos
and the best sex
while eating burritos
and running with scissors
is the only way to make danger understand
that whatever point it's trying to make,
I'm only three-eighths listening
23 percent of the time
and won't be its minion
or sock puppet. The rest is gravy
if it's mashed potatoes day.
By my watch, it's quarter past
let's get on with singing the tuba parts
if we have to, if not all the Muses
can come out to play.
There are two of us here
and that's a quorum
if one lights the match
and one seconds the motion.

## Amen

There's no one I'll touch
who isn't a killer, of bugs or squirrels or convicts
by the proxy of law, but some creatures
have the countervirtue of softness: decades

my days have begun with fur, petting a dog
seventeen years, two cats twelve, the remaining cat
two more, daughter of the cat who died
and is buried under a rock I also pet in the dark
to hear it purr. I asked science is there a way

I can hold a human heart to my ear and harmonize
with the sky implicit in its voice; science said no,
but isn't dry ice cool? Intimacy is the surmounting

of physical limitations by physical means,
whether fingertips or vowels or the earth-eyes
of a dog, and when a movie says men don't need it,
I know it was written by a lumberjack
trying to pretend he doesn't apologize on his knees
to the stumps of trees. The softest of softnesses

in my life has a rain forest for a mouth, is how it feels
in certain moments, such as every time my wife grasps
the hardest part of me and does this sexy thing
with her tongue: speaks.

## A visit to my pantheon reveals a hole in the sky

My body's been traveling fifty-eight years
to look at the light of as many stars
as I can devour on the same night I learn
Maggie Roche died last year and I didn't cry
or lay a white dress on the snow
to commemorate her shyness.
Even if you don't know who she was
or can't hold a tune or started using
meth again after promising yourself
no more falling down the stairs,
I hope you're kissed tonight
for real, not like people at midnight on TV
pretending time is a dog
we've taught to sit. I think I mean
we scream Happy New Year
as if we can tell the future
what to do, trying hard to look
as if we feel the way champagne tastes,
and I don't believe for a second
we've got such beautifully lit
chandeliers inside us. My resolution's
to leave Roche sister albums
and turntables lying around the universe
for people to hear a more reasonable version
of joy, harmonies congregating
around the language of insurmountable distance,
people who'll come home
and gather a child or man or ukulele
or mountain in their arms
and hold tighter to knowing everything
we get now is a give
on the other end, for I am indeed

a wistful motherfucker, as predicted
by the sky of my birth and noted
by Denis Johnson after I read poems
decades ago in Kalamazoo, when he was still
what the living call incredible and I said
*I'm sorry, I couldn't hear you,*
just to make him say again
that little thing we ask of life,
that a god or anyone
notice us at all.

Do you spell *role model* role model or roll model?

Some people seem to have eaten nothing
but dignity their whole lives. I'm thinking
of Bill Russell, he of the laugh that belongs
in the Museum of Gracious Sounds.
There's the obvious stuff to admire:
he made defense sexy, which is like making dirt
a hit on the runways of Milan; won eleven
NBA titles in Boston, a town famous for tea
and its love of tall black men; worked and walked
with Malcolm X; was on *Sesame Street*. More difficult
to measure or praise is fluidity, the ability to move
from a comment about the beating of a boy
just trying to cross a street, to giggling
over Red Auerbach's cigar, before sliding
to a consideration of the athlete as property. Granted
I know him only through the voyeur of TV,
but he's always felt more electric and layered
than the celebrities I'm supposed to covet
and inject, more calm and reasonable,
perhaps the man above all others I hope never
to meet. What stammering, falling-down thing
would I say? And what if he's got bad breath
or hates dogs or snaps at a personal assistant
who has to call him *O Center of My Universe*
over the number of marshmallows in his cocoa?
I like him with me this way—a man I see
or think of several times a year, who never fails
to compel me to believe our species, in addition
to suicidal tendencies and greed, has grace
and the promise of greater grace to come. Who cares
if I'm wrong about him or us? If the apple's
too high in the tree? If time's

just a measure of heat, which is dissipating,
drifting off and leaving us to fend
with knowing everything we see or are, every concept
or hope we have of heaven, will collapse
into a dot too small to refer to kindly
as a speck of dust? Bill Russell took on the giant
Wilt Chamberlain and won, took on Southie
and survived, took on age and looked good
at eighty-three on TV last night, still
with the quickest trigger finger on a laugh
I've ever known, a dead-shot joy. So bring it on,
entropy, Tuesday morning, hatred, nihilism,
impenetrable fortresses of power and inscrutable
billing for knee surgery—do your worst
and I'll do my best and we'll see
who's standing naked tonight in the yard
being pawed by the thin light of stars.
That'll be me here and you there
and everyone else
wherever they've got enough sense
to keep trying to be touched
in a cosmos growing colder all the time,
if you want to get technical and tell the truth.

# A meditation on hoarding

Last Wednesday I murdered a bat
with a window screen. It was in the house
and swooping around and around
like my worry that I have neither
a porpoise or a purpose,
until I felt I had to knock it down
to get it outside and save it
from the madness of a dwelling
that has no sky in it. I didn't realize
how tender bats are. It looked tiny
on the floor and delicate as a note
folded and passed from a boy to a girl
in fourth grade that he likes her
and will she marry him at lunch?
She did, and they lived happily together
until the end of school that day.
I was the boy the boy who wrote that note
asked are there two rs in marry.
Spelling matters, as does the feeling
I'm under a spell of breathing
I don't want to end. Part of me
expects to look up one night
and find a tombstone where my favorite star
was, the same part that got stoned and drunk
and tied string around everything
on the first floor of a house in Grand Rapids
with John-whose-last-name-escapes-me,
around chairs and fixtures and the toaster
and doorknobs and the piano,
as if holding the world together
wasn't just for spiders anymore but a job
for a man with no qualifications

other than the suicide that was often
on his mind but hasn't been for years.
Killing me is cancer's job, not mine.
It might sound funny, but I don't think
about death nearly as much
as my poems do: before the sun comes up,
I give death a chance to breathe,
and for the rest of the day, try to pile up
as much as I can to miss.

## Just checking in

Do you believe the speculation
that soon, having already fought over land,
God, beets, the size of your crown
versus my crown, we'll be fighting
over water, the right to raise roses
and bathe and live? The pessimist in me
wears a suit of armor and says Yes,
while the optimist is too busy
staring at the sun to take this survey.
They are inseparable as dust
and sneezing. Where one goes,
the other says, Watch out. And when one says,
A random-number generator
has more to look forward to
than I do, the other says,
It's as if my soul were eating rat poison
when I read that Bechtel owns the rights
to rain in Bolivia. Would you go to jail
for putting a bucket on your roof?
More importantly, would I? I need to know
so I can arrange bail now. Never put off
until tomorrow preparations
for Armageddon you can do today,
said my pappy, right before telling me
to never call him pappy again.
My all-time favorite question
in school was, What are the results
of a zero-sun game? Second place
went to, Is history a measure
of progress or the increasing noise
of a system going to ruin? My answers
were Eight and Yes. My laughter

was recorded and sent into space.
My crying was famous
for frightening rocks away. What else
can I tell you about me: I'm scared
but not shitless. Eager
though incapable of wagging. Here
but also there. Trying. I am trying
your patience and to make it
to the other side, wherever that is.

## You say potato, I say enough

There was a flittingness to language
long ago, the word for sun, say,
changing to *souleil, soulet,*
*soulot, s'lot, slu, soureil, s'reil,*
*seroille* every few kilometers
as you crawled or bounded
east to west along the Côte d'Azur,
thinking of your *père* or *papo,*
saying *oui* or *bai* to a glass of wine,
whatever it was called
wherever you stood, a democracy
of speech found everywhere,
not just France, a fecundity
reduced to unity over time, as village
was eaten by city by nation
by TV. I always want to be a butterfly

when I'm watching a butterfly,
or the moon when I'm a butterfly
looking at the moon, or a river
when I'm the moon
shining a light on the night
all alone, so pay no attention
to my solitude, as it doesn't even know
where it belongs or what to call itself,
right now or in the future, standing here
or sitting there or falling
wherever I'll fall. And this nostalgia

for a time when *tongue* or *love*
was reborn place to place, into diphthongs
and phonemes I couldn't imagine

unless I had an affair with a linguist,
was also a time when a stranger
could be hacked apart for owning
an unknown face, and talking
in a manner that reminded people
the devil was overdue and sure to sound
as if he were arguing with the air;
the hacking, far from crime,
was a public good, a service
to everything that mattered,
the husband or wife or child
who could be lost any moment, just like now,
with no words to make sense of loss
even in the province of my head,
that placeless place, that land
I never leave but never find
the heart of, despite the wanderings,
maps, bread crumbs, dictionaries, the crying,
most of it silent, the laughing, most of it
at the crying man in my head, the wheezing,
the big gobs of snot, and that crying face
that looks like a casino being imploded
in Vegas, or a rose taking a shit,
or whatever nonhuman comparison
you care to make in your village of one
to this most human thing.

## Poem for the left hand

What is it about poetry
that it refuses to die
no matter how often
TV shoots it in the head?

Must be the minty fresh breath
of the soul, the crinkle-crinkle
of the candy wrapper of the soul,
the high cheekbones
and debutante posture
of the soul, must be the soul
of the owl inside all of us
spinning its head around
like a lazy Susan
or an energetic Susan
or a compass with eyes
in the back of its eyes
trying to point the way home.

Home is where the Wi-Fi is.

Home is the feeling
your mud-wrestling days
are over.

Who can pin mud anyway?

Who can explain lonely
to ants?

Poetry will last as long
as there's a woman in the corner
with her back to the party

building a piano out of matches
so she can explain to the humans
she resembles in shape though not
flammability that splayed
and broken is the beginning
of harmonic and blessed.

Shiver

Cold nights make me think
of frozen bagels versus fresh
versus my warm bed versus sleeping
and dying under the overpass
sounding impossibly tragically
funny to me, like overruling
the undertow or high-fiving
the guy who lowballed his offer
on your collection of hawk feathers
and string. In the Museum
of Horrible Outcomes,
the *Unfettered Capitalism* exhibit
runs from sea to shining
and slowly deoxygenated sea,
and includes human beings
in popsicle form, about which
the docents have been trained
to say, *Fuck yes bad things happen*
*to good people, right on*
*right on right on. Anyway.* And then
you move on to shiny stuff
like the Porsche 911 Walt Whitman drove
while writing *Leaves of Grass*
*My Ass, Leave My Shit Alone,*
that most American of poems
about the un-American dream
I pray we wake from
any day now and say *Now what*
*the hell was that?*

## Tough-guy talk

She hugged my paper route.

I slept with her telescope full of stars.

She put my yo-yo on her wedding finger.

We rolled down a hill, one on top of one
on bottom on top of the grass & laugh
of the other.

When we stood up we were twenty-two.

We're the same—she likes and I like
girls & that we like girls
under the same moon
in two time zones with still
a tin-can-telephone string
between us.

I'm ready to be her best man
if you're ready to let two shes
get hitched in Lubbock,
dear Texas.

She smelled like a swing set.

I punched her once in the hair.

What do you care if two dykes
share a life, even underwear?

How cool is that—one thong
for all and all of us thronging
for one thing—love.

She sat beside my sitting
beside her chucking stones
on the curb at the other side
of the world, wanting to be old
and get our hands on the controls.

How cute is dumb we were, plumb wrong
in our hurry to get up and out
we were: I miss going to the river
and pretending it was land
that rolled away, miss everything
about our short days, but that's
the point of memory, isn't it—the lure
of pure?

Texas, I'm slipping my tux on
and coming.

By the time I get there, you better be
a real he-man and give everyone
the chance to be equal to every other
befuddled mother father sister brother—
that is, everyone officially afraid
of being alone, with a ring on
that doesn't ring to prove it.

Or else—so there, take that—
I'll cry.

## Nature versus murmur

Guy sleeping soundly on the sidewalk
on the west side of the portrait gallery
in DC—people thronging by, going home
or to Zaytinya, fantastic food
from Lebanon, Turkey, Greece—barefoot—
the guy, not the fattoush—ugly toenails,
like oatmeal dried under a heat lamp
and hammered as far away from symmetry
as possible—though his hands were folded
under his right cheek in a cliché
of sleepy peace—I consider him a relative
of the pileated woodpecker—a statistically rare
but not infrequent sight—one of those things
in wrong places we accept—ships in bottles—
crooks in office—nipples on men—yes,
I noticed that word too—*thing*—and want
to verb it—the *thinging* of people
is slow—like arsenic—poison
you can be slipped in littles
without getting hip to your imminent demise—
the homeless shock wears off—the tendency
to reach and offer—to think of my own bed
and three sets of sheets, all the same color
because I'm boring—it's just, you know,
a dude sleeping on the street
a few blocks from the White House—
no biggie—and what would I do anyway—
give a shit?—buy him some tzatziki,
which was great?—the lentil doohickeys,
not so much—I'm eating a bowl of raisin bran
trying to finish this poem—the cereal's
just there on top of the fridge—the fridge

just there in the kitchen—the kitchen
just there in the dream of my life—
though I am nowhere you are not—
how do I orient myself to the universe,
I am asking—is it a matter
of falling in love with something small
like dust or vast like the totality
of gestures the desperate, the clingy atoms
make—I thought at the start of this
I'd be helpful or insightful—
in one erased passage, I invoked de Tocqueville—
in another, there was a peacock,
the Statue of Liberty, a transcription
of "Fanfare for the Common Man"
into commas and exclamation points—
but here I am, turning to you, asking,
can you help me out—lend me
some understanding of how I could walk
by this guy not once but twice—
not in some future but this life—
not in theory but in fact—without—
that's it—without

## There's no i in unity after the first i

"My Way" should only be sung underwater,
so the narcissism is softened a bit
by drowning. It's not really Frank Sinatra
I want to pick on but the lack of applause
for collective effort. "We did it our way"
would be among the least American lyrics
ever written, for reasons John Wayne made clear
every time he sashayed onto screen and fed
our love of a big man solving a big problem
with a gun. I am the lone wolf
of the solitary song of my soul, the good cop
working against a corrupt system
of pipes and valves or however it is
that the sludge of government flows. I am an eagle
soaring to a swell of violins above a mountain,
though if you listen closely, that sound I make
in every movie and TV show, that piercing,
majestic screech, is really the call
of a hawk: even this bit of iconic individuality
is a team effort. Eagles actually make
this pitiful cheeping sound; I'm no good
at public speaking; I've seen your work
in avant-garde haberdashery and it's atrocious;
but if it's pie we want, you take the filling,
I'll handle the crust, or a table we need,
you've got an appetite and I've got a tree
that lightning chopped down, or an orgy
you're after, by definition
that demands a mess of legs and arms
and torsos and the other stuff,
the hugging and kissing and stroking,
the trying to light the match

of one body against another,
on the off-chance we can be alone together
long enough to forget this doesn't last.

## Encore

At the rehab center
late at night when my father
presses the call button,
someone hurries in
and shuts it off, thus maintaining
their quick-response rate, but leaves
without helping him pee, he tells me
in a whisper on the best
spring day of the year so far,
of the century: I could have picked
two hundred
million snowdrops on the way in
had I patience
and a doll's fingers.          He's afraid

of angering the staff and has learned to pee
on himself with dignity.          It's all

in the not-crying.          In imagining

he's a chunk of wind
the next day while his penis
is being washed
and he can't feel it, just a sock
with a hole in it.          I'm afraid

of the future.          That I'll need a gun

to help me out of the jam
of having a body.          Is what I'm thinking

while holding his hand, while believing
there's nothing to be done

about the weight of the night
on his chest except to lift him
and carry him home and give him back
to his own bed to live and die in,
as he and my mother
gave me to the sun all those years ago
to run under and end up here,
not knowing what to do
about the rumor that part of us
goes on after the heart's last sigh,
other than applaud the possibility
as I would a woman
standing up from a piano
after the gazelles of her hands
have stopped running, the music over
but not the chance for more music
if we clap enough that she believes
how desperate we are and that only
she can save us.

## Unto the breach

After five days of hydrocodone for kidney stones,
five days I didn't bathe, read the Magna Carta,
or poop, a man reached in and emptied my rectum,
one of the greatest kindnesses ever shown me,
so civil, I expected to look up and see him
in a tux, headed out to hear or even meet
Philip Glass, creator of "Music in the Shape
of a Square," which I listen to with stubbornly
loopy ears, and cried softly through my thank-yous
as he did so, like rain that wants to remain
on the grass, to fall no farther from the sun
than the tip of every blade, the top
of all the green reaching toward the future,
the dream I've been having and asking my body
to share, the boat of me I keep wrecking, the room
I never asked to enter and will only leave once,
what other metaphors fail to capture the truth
of anything, let alone the fact of home, the shape
I hold but am not, the matter I've borrowed
but mutter on about as my own, as if I possess
any of the roses I've ever given your hand
to marry for as long as beauty pretends to want us.

## Zing

To this day I like licking nine-volts, the zots
from the cold metal poles and am sorry a little bit
that licking my wife isn't like that, a little bit
that air isn't one hundred and twenty volts, that I can't
plug my table saw into a cloud. On the other hand,
I haven't tried. Haven't opened a window in a plane
and reached into this possible communication.
Or said to a doctor, how can an enlarged heart
be a bad thing, such as yesterday at the hospital
when my mom's swollen ticker afforded me the chance
to interject thus. I have to tell you my wife
won't like the start of this poem. Or when her grandmother
dies. Or when drought kills her flowers, even if I tell her
it's an evolution to tatters I find lovelier
than when the breeze was lithe with the currents
of their blooms, but I may not be the best judge of beauty
or anything. I lick batteries, remember. It's like electroshock
for cowards. Like practicing French-kissing lightning
or American-kissing thunder, a jolt of enthusiasm,
spritz of wake-up sent arrowing to the brain.
Mine lives in a cave with the lights off. Is that why sorrow
grows like mold? God I have questions. Why don't zealots
see how boring they are? Does birdsong
really travel better in morning air? Answers
will arrive in pieces that may or may not resemble
the whole. And one day when I shiver, it'll be my skin
feeling your eyes walking across this poem.

## Say uncle

Along the way, he stopped caring
for sleep—whether he had morphine
or bologna for lunch—
whether the birthday cake
was made with flour
or flowers—he just wanted
to play his violin—
the one they buried with him—
the one his father carried
out of Minsk before the war—play
for the old cancer woman
across the street—for himself—
for the curtains
and the wind in the curtains—
I brought him a cup of tomato soup
once, he asked me to drink it
and tell the authorities
he had, and while I helped him lie,
he played a tune
that sounded like me
catching frogs along the Grand River,
as if my past
were a little bird
he'd watched and watched
cross the sky—
it's hard for me to say
he starved himself to death
in French or Spanish,
otherwise I'm happy
he left when and how
he wanted—his violin
is with him

but not his bow—
he gave it to me
instead of money,
which flies away—
instead of a cow,
which runs out of milk—
instead of crying,
which has no purpose
other than rust—
I touch it now and then
to my ear—almost
in the way I let snow
brush against me
and remind me I am not
the world but a thing
the world holds

## As a translator I'm a pretty good turtle

The rain sounds like a child taking a bath.

We're at a kitchen table translating Arash's poem
from Farsi,
which I don't know, to English, which he hardly speaks.

So far what's clear is we both like tennis,
that there are too many English words for gun, that his daughter
needs to put a plastic turtle on my bald head
because we look related, and that I have to pretend
I know something about war or his poem will sound
like his daughter isn't missing an eye, like everyone lived.

So I ask him to draw what it felt like, the day the poem
was born, and he snaps a pencil doing so, which makes me wonder
if I have anything to offer as a friend, if a bucket,
dropped down the well of my mouth, would ever reach water.

We stop when the only line he asks his wife about
makes her leave the room, makes him follow, and when he comes back,
he touches his words and asks how we say…
then makes a fist and explodes it into an open hand
above his heart.

How do I say we've never known how to say that:

burn a dictionary in front of him, sharpen the pencil
and make it bleed while drawing a truer face
on my face, cut a hole in the roof and live there
under the rain, the touch of sky, ask him to beat me to death
and offer the same, beg him to carry me in his eyes
as far as he can look us away from this life?

I worry for him and his daughter and his wife,
for everyone when it's this easy to bring war
to a place of bread, but Arash wants his poem to live
in two languages, and this turtle will do his best
to give it that second mouth.

## Waiting is the hardest part of waiting

I like the way your nose wrinkles
when you confuse a coping saw
for a coping mechanism and cut a duck

out of balsa to float on the lake and keep
the mallard with one wing company
badly, in that your duck has the shape

and soul of a potato. Though who cares
if you had shop or not,
if the potato-duck catches on

as a species—you're to be cheered
for making a mess in the garage
while waiting for the results of the test

that'll answer the big question, is there a riot
in your cells? Which if there is,
I'm afraid of the saws they'll turn on you,

of the masked ones who cut and gut, cut and run,
leaving you aching and waiting to know
if the cancer's gone or just kicked a bit

in the balls. Which has no bearing
whatsoever on the duck, the duck stuck
when the others leave

with us, who don't even have the one wing
to suggest the other wing
we also don't have, if you get my meaning,

let me know, because I'm lost.

## Exhaling

The whistling language of Aas
was dead fifteen years
before people outside the village
knew it had existed, seventy
before I read of it
after reading some Darwish poems
and wondering whether he liked doves
or deer more. I'm proud
that the current group of deer
in my yard stay when I go out
to pet the white cat who adopted us
and is blind in one eye, as I am blind
when it comes to the past: whether it's an owl
or piece of spiderweb
stuck in my hair, I don't know.
I wanted to be moved
so read the poems, wanted to know
all the ways we've talked to one another
so read the book, wanted to change
the shape of my mind
so started typing and am sad
that up to now I've hidden
behind interesting people and facts
and not told the truth,
that I woke up at three
and got out of bed at four
to ask my breath
why it won't let me go,
why it keeps wearing my chest
when I know it could be out there
with sparrows and clouds, sunwarmed
or splashing rain across its face.

That we're instances of wind
never leaves my mind,
especially when I'm drunk
or sober or tall or getting shorter
all the time, we shrink
as we age and age
as the number of people we try to carry
grows, I have twenty
in my hands right now
and they're not that big,
about the size of the galaxy
when I extend them into the night, light-years
between my left and right.
The whistlers could be heard
two miles away, raising the question
is everything we say
a measure of distance, *cup*
or *window* or *love* the gap
between water and thirst,
seeing and doubt, freezing
and a sky that's been a roof
over my head for years, protecting me
from having to look up
and not make sense
of a completely different dream,
one in which the sun rises
over a tugboat and not a mountain,
or has eight stars
where there's nothing now,
an absence I adore
for the expectation
of what desire will make
of that open space, a space
the shape of everything
it isn't.

## Sweet

My habit in December is to peel an orange
as I walk—bits of peel in my pockets—
pants that smell of Florida—and sometimes
approach a car at an intersection—
tap on the window—interrupt
the driver's rapture of watching
for the green light of release—I'm sworn at
by most—flipped off—or ignored
with the same passion with which I'm ignored by God—
but she rolled down her window
when I made the motion of a crank
with my hand—took the half I offered—
the sweetness of a warmer sky—
and ate the slices in front of me—with me—
as I my equal measure devoured—then left
our common life together—the only moment
of our eternal bond—the link
that will play out as a long string
between us, no matter what pleasure
is advanced by other days—we looked
at each other and ate bits of a world
making the most of the sun—of the light
that is blowing away into nothingness—
the moment so small, so precise,
it was easy to love everything
we knew of each other—I had a gift
and she had a desire
to accept that gift—we were whole—
we were cured—had advanced
the cause of being
ever so slightly along the path
it wanders with us, little bits of dust
caught in its hair

## Civilization

We were going along. Holding
hands. When we came across a man
punching another man. My lover's
a creature wired with surprising
windings, and noticed the man
doing the punching looked tired.
She offered and was accepted
in her offer to punch the other man
for the punching man awhile.
Then gave me a look that said,
*Where are your manners?*
and I donated the punched man
my body to be his body
for a period of time. During
this rest, they took a tender
interest in each other, asking
after children and spouses
and bets on long-shot horses,
even sharing a ham sandwich
one had kept hidden & warm
under his arm. When they ran out
of things to say, rather than accept
the onslaught of silence, the one
tapped her shoulder and the other
mine. To his *thank you*, I said
a bloody *you're welcome* as we
walked off again holding hands.
Of all the reasons I love
my love, not the least is
she knows how the world works.
Badly. Etiquette is the way
she fights back. And with a right cross

I can tell you from experience
is lovely. My head still rings
from how considerate she is.

The dichotomy lobotomy

In the old argument
over left versus right, nature
versus rapture, nurture versus murmur,
bullet versus ballot, ballot
versus mallet, power
versus sharing, money
versus gimme gimme gimme, screaming
versus what did you say,
I try to listen to both sides
of the wind as I pedal my bike
up a mountain to see
what I can see. Which is trees,
mostly. Trees up close
and in the distance, trees.
Green here and green there
and green green green
between. All under a hat
of blue sky. Versus, hearses, curses:
nothing good rhymes
with versus. Nurses, I guess.
Nurses with purses.
I was wrong. Humility
versus humidity. Ears
versus jeers. Love
is to livid as kissing is
to pissing on. Middle ground
versus middle finger.

## One for all

Incarceration. *In- carcer:* in prison. *Carcer,*
from *karkros:* barrier. From *kr-kr-:* circular.
Yet little in prison is round. Little
in prison is round. In prison is round. Prison
is round. Is round. Round.

Is round round?

From the sun we get circle, get grass
and touching in grass while our touching
is touched by grass in a ring of intimacy,
if you're lucky and not in prison. I am lucky
and not in prison. White and lucky and not
in prison. White in person and personable
at a distance, not in person. Not in person
is personally the only way I'd want to be
in prison, with its impersonal, rectangular,
angular insistence on in not getting out.

Is America addicted to slavery? Today,
I am a color swatch. Rest me against a wall
or sky. Put me in your pocket. Carry me
to Angola. Go cell to cell.
Call every this man forward. Call every that man
friend and ask if he wants to be compared
to freedom. I am freedom. Freedom
is a brownish, pinkish chalk. Is mostly
totally relative. As in my relatives
arrived on the right boats. My relatives
weren't slaves but indentured servants.
One giant step closer to being thought of
as human. Call prisons what they are: dark places
holding darkness.

They want to build another prison. They being
them. Them being us. Us being the objective case
of we. The objective case being, I object. I
to the we. I to the nth degree to the more.
I object to the object. The prison. I want not
the not-circle. I object. I bone, skin, thigh.
*The ideal*, Plato wrote, *is to eat all your chicken.*
*The idea*, Carl Jung wrote, *is we dream what we are.*
*The id*, Frankenstein wrote, *is an ugly dress to wear.*
*The I*, I am writing to the future of this sentence,
*is responsible for thunder.* The I so solitarily
confined. So concertina wired. The I trying to break out
of the I. I object to mandatory minimum sentences.
I want mandatorily maximum sentences
of wisteria and flying and the end
of the War on Drugs and the obliteration
of the war on people. I want a war
on color as crime, on poverty as sin, on sin
as the state of being we're in. I want. I need.
I jones. The itch of my itch of my yen of my lean
of my fall of my cower of my flutter of my fathom
of my dive of my rise: to unprison myself
from myself. To be naked with the them
that is us that is I, to be simply
and equally here and human. Can America
be addicted to freedom in time?

In zoo news today

Animals have trusted me.
However else I've failed
to make it to the Olympics,
fold a flag properly,
resolve or even understand
tensions in the Middle East,
animals have trusted me. A few of them
human. One of them human. One half
of one of them human. The rest of her,
I don't know what she is. I'm thinking
an otter floating on its back
in Monterey Bay, smashing
abalone open with a rock. If you sit
still long enough, hummingbirds
will come right up to your nose
to see if it's a flower.
It's not, in case you're wondering,
enough to say first do no harm,
you have to first do no harm
and second do no damage and third
stick your hand out for new dogs
to sniff. In another life
I was a dog who thought
in another life I was a person
who thought in another life
I was better at whatever this is.
Going, this is, so fast
I often want to put on the brakes
and hug an elephant or what else
feels as big as desire feels? Whales
are the only other corollary,
and did I just call the love

of my life half an otter? I apologize.
She's full-bore, full-tilt otter.
And abalone: sorry. And time:
slow down. Put your feet up. Please.

## The outer inner self

I have a horn growing from my forehead. Like my worst habits, it's invisible to me. These include yelling at crickets to shut up. Apparently I do this in my sleep. I've been hoping to build a cathedral in my sleep. How cool would it be to wake up to Notre-Dame on the front lawn? You don't have to say *very*. The *very* is implied by your existence. Any reasonable person is in awe of large buildings created to meet God. As it's impossible to meet God, the buildings are incarnations of our desire to do the impossible. The horn grows down and over my nose. A lover once drew a sketch for me. I loved watching her hand. It was muscled and veiny and seemed to think for itself. Her face scrunched while she worked. She looked like a rose struggling to bloom. Concentration is its own little room. No windows or doors. I get that way kneading bread. I often look up from kneading bread and realize it's changed from summer to winter. She liked the horn. The dancer liked the horn. The nurse liked the horn. I've dated many women who do interesting things. They all believed the horn was a confession—the horn is me admitting I'm ugly inside and not trying to hide it. But they're all gone and the horn is here. This is worrisome to think about metaphorically. It suggests I'm married to the horn. That there's no escape from the self. But what better use of escape hatches than the self? Don't say submarine. That's the obvious choice. Say cloud. Say fire. Say if you could open your shadow, you'd jump through.

## About the size of it

A little bird lands on a little branch
on a big tree on a little piece of land
my once big but shrinking father owns
in a big country that sits between two other
big countries on a small planet
with two big oceans, one bigger and meaner
than the other, a goldfinch I want to encourage
to follow me everywhere I go or let me
follow it everywhere it goes, though lacking gestures
both big and small and words both big and small
to transmit this encouragement from my bigger
to its smaller brain, I take the little while
the big sky has offered us together
as a present of indeterminate size I need
to open now, before the little idea
of a little bird flies away from my mind,
as my littler and littler father looks up
and points at the little shimmer on the little branch
and reaches through the big holes in his thoughts
for the sounds that mean *I am happy the universe*
*has included me in its grasp,* or *pretty bird*
if you must get a little technical, his face
looking like a bigger and bigger hole in the air
when the words won't come, with me a little useless
and largely pointless beside him, my breath
shuttling in and out, as if it can't decide
between stay and go, the little bird
long gone by the time I realize
the sun has set and it will soon feel
like my father was never here, which is no big deal
compared to the erasures the world endures
every day, except this one is mine.

## Still

There's laughter in slaughter

I didn't see this coming
when 12 were shot
when 21 when 27
when I was a boy by a river
better than the Seine
at whetting my appetite
for rivers

then I wrote *slaughter*
on a legal pad
and for the first time wondered,
*Are there illegal pads?*
and noticed the sick message
in the bottle of the word
and decided language
is the funniest thing
the cruelest April
I've ever put in my mouth

when 32 were shot
when 50
when the daily 1s and 2s
piled up I grew immune
to the measles but not this

I've written versions of this poem
as long as I've asked a pen to help me
be a better person
at falling down
at whispering to genitals
at going to Montreal

at cutting boards
into smaller boards
to make a house of what trees
do naturally

eventually I realized
the poems are all horrible
especially this poem
especially the next poem
due any tomorrow now
because rain
won't fall up
cats won't come
when dogs call them
Americans won't stop
ordering fries
with a side of .45s
and I won't give up
on the faith
of the Romantics
that a gentleman
always brings semantics
to a gunfight

## Θαλασσόπλαγκτος, or why didn't someone ask me sooner?

My plan was to be happy and write about a Greek word
that means "made to wander over the sea"
if I could learn how to type it in my old version
of WordPerfect, but I made a mistake and looked
at Google News: the Ohio legislature has approved a law
banning abortions once a fetal heartbeat can be heard,
or six weeks in most cases. Now I'm stuck, as politics
and poetry get along about as well as lips
and soldering irons, hawks and wet cement;
and amazing clouds are just now rolling past
the mountain I sit in front of every morning,
wide spaced and red as pomegranates on the bottom,
each a kind of boat; and I'm incapable
of the Vulcan mind-meld, which would allow me
to put my hand on a stranger's face and perhaps
understand why anyone wants to tell anyone else
what to do. I don't even want to tell myself
what to do, making me a horrible state senator
from Ohio or Greek king who condemns a man
to live in a boat on the sea and have moussaka
and retsina no more, but I don't think it's my biz
whether my jizz ultimately becomes a tot or not,
since I'm not the one who has to slosh around
nine months with a wee fish inside my wee ocean.
If I heard one three hundred eighty-ninth
the concern for the sacredness of life
once the kid has popped and needs grub
and love and shoes and shots, once there's more
than a lub-dub in the tummy, I'd at least
be impressed by the moral consistency
of the vision, but usually those insistent
on nixing a woman's say on whether

she creates a human being, won't give a fig
or farthing to the living
once they've imbibed actual air.
It's clear the solution's to never read
the news before I write, never live
in Ohio, never be or love a woman
who wants to steer her own ship, Greek or not.
Problem solved, easy peasy, what's next?

# End of the work ethic

(alternate title:
If Mick Jagger didn't exist,
we'd have to invent him)

(alternate alternate title:
I am old and afraid)

Bum left foot. Gimpy right hip
& knee, elbow & shoulder. Blown-out
left groin. Also dizzy a lot.
The shooting pains
of self-doubt. But Stratocasters
don't smash themselves.
Every night, I get up on stage
and make love with my rage. Not
that you notice. I see you out there
yawning, checking for texts,
your face haloed
in phone-glow. You used to prefer
the lyrics of my narcissism
to yours. I should quit.
Raise llamas or alpacas or whatever
those weird animals are
who look like sheep
trying to be horses. Anyway,
there's no such thing
as a rock 'n' roll comb-over.
All those pills. All that blood
and cum. I got so much empty
inside me, if you dropped a pebble
in my mouth, you'd never hear it
hit bottom. I won't even

tell myself when I'm doing
my last show. I'll find out
like everyone else—when I read
the suicide note.

## Ticktock

The beautiful thing about time—beyond walking
along the Grand River while carrying it in my pocket
with bubble gum and lint—or measuring it
by folding a piece of paper into a triangle
and teaching my nephew how the length of the sides
whisper to each other, *If you will forever*
*be* t, *I will forever be* t *times the square root*
*of two*—what romance, what devotion
compared to my refrigerator reneging each week
on the promise to feed me—the stunning thing
about time is how it brushes its hair
disguised as a woman leaning over a basin
on a hill above the Mediterranean, the window open
as I count the strokes, getting as high
as one and starting over, leaving me always
at the beginning of her hand treating her life
as a loom—as I have treated my life
as the only leg I have to stand on
and the only mouth I'll ever get
to open in a moon-shape or close
around her nipples and feel blood
rushing toward the warmth
and asking to be touched

## For you alone

One knows the world is falling
slightly faster than rising,
this is why one has the second beer
or tries to stretch the triple
into a love affair. One is called out
at home and asks the ump
how anyone can know anything
for sure and is told it's the little hat
the umpire wears that makes all
the epistemological difference
in the world. One is pleased
by this news and the tails of comets
and the various enthusiasms of children
in playgrounds when they gather
their shrieks into a single
ululation holding up the sky.
One knows the sky is not actually
held up by this joy but one needs
to take a stab at meaning before meaning
takes a swing at one. One dreams
of less violence for oneself and others
and of growing old with a cane
because one wants to think
one is standing in the middle
of a great party, or that osprey
are pending, or that love
something something. One says a lot
that makes little sense, like one believes
in peace an hour before one wants
to punch the secretary of defense
in the nose. But one
can only speak for oneself

and others and people
who don't exist and dogs.

## Hope (testicular cancer)

for Matt Cunningham

Mourning doves on the cedar planters I made last year
cooing and shitting like they were invited
to remind me I'm alive by the sun climbing the mountains
a little more to the north every day. Pulling out a bent nail

early and not angering it into place like I would have
when I was ten. Ocracoke being hard to get to

with its root beer floats and stories of shipwrecks I survive
every time. A lover who is sexy counting your lonely ball

over and over in the seventeen languages she knows
to count to one in. Blood delivering oxygen to the garden

of my body. The shed I'm building for shovels and wood
and shadows. The poem I'm building for my mind

to have a window to look out of. My mother

coming home from the hospital with third-stage
liver disease instead of fourth, with a partially
collapsed lung instead of an announcement in the paper.
That two balls means you've been carrying a spare. I knew

this guy who had cancer, they kept cutting chunks of him out,
he'd return with absences inside and build a birdhouse
for each one, his mornings surrounded by the most musical air
he could breathe. Beyond such diligent fury

to live and the obsession of atoms to cloud in the shape
of my wife's face and the moon following us with its slow
winking eye and the word *Scheherazade* sounding like slipping naked

down a water slide and lightning being a show-off with the spiky rivers
of its artistry and tractors bringing us wheat with steel
that could have been rifles and the ferocious salvation
of chemo and the cool breeze that just rose a hand to my face
and said, Get on with it: beyond these things, there's nothing more

than more of these things, in my experience, from where I sit
wondering have you leaned a little to one side
since the operation and will you tell your children
of your ghost ball decades from now and that you were afraid
you wouldn't have the chance to meet them but then woke
and crawled out of the cave of anesthesia and the world
asked you to stay and you did.

## Baby steps

Long ago, my father began dressing himself
for his death. He didn't trust anyone else
with the task. He also dug the hole,
gathered the flowers, and cried
while talking about what a great
and kind man he was. He got very good
at not blushing during the eulogy
and not complaining when dirt was dropped
on his head. He went on living
as he was dying and dying as he was living,
always prepared, always thorough,
but never once chased a butterfly
that I knew of. It might have happened,
since parents have these secret lives
children don't know about—doors
they walk through hidden in bookcases
and mistresses disguised as infatuations
with model trains—but joy isn't a hat
I ever saw him wear. He was too busy
labeling his label gun LABEL GUN
to let down the hair he'd never grow
over his ears in case it'd keep him
from hearing death's approach. Death
which rides a horse or drives a stick
or has a go-kart—who really knows?
When my father finally died,
we didn't notice,
as he'd been practicing
for years. He
was like the boy who cried wolf
or squid or avalanche.
And since he'd want me

to learn from his life, I've tried
to be the boy who cries Yippee
and does a wheelie, even when
his hovercraft is in the shop.

## If it's not fixable, don't break it

The neighbors with a little pond
filled in the little pond.
The frogs bothered them.
The rhythmic sexual thrum
of wanting to get laid,
wanting to go on being frogs
with a purity of focus
I can only dream of bringing
to the essential work of my species,
which vacillates between killing
everything we see and trying
to have a conversation with clouds.
But the frogs won in the end.
Or in the middle, since the parade
isn't over. Water came back.
Water got down on one knee,
looked over the land and realized
that for all the hubbub, my neighbors
are not civil engineers:
there was still a bowl
where there had been a bowl,
just a different bowl,
and water respects all bowls
equally. Then water did
what it was raised from a pup
to do—flowed and filled.
After which the frogs
resumed their calling
of doing it. For by doing it,
it will have been done.
And it having been done,
they can move on

to the important task
of doing it again.
My breathing agrees
100 percent
with this philosophy.
Over and over, in with the fire,
out with the ashes.
In with the shimmery aura
surrounding every little heartbeat
and twig, out with a riderless horse
crossing the snow.
Where death fails,
humping succeeds.
That's all rock 'n' roll
has been saying.

## We've come a long way toward getting nowhere

My obsession with Jews is an obsession
with one Jew. I look at her walking
and wonder what anyone could have
against Jews, at her sleeping
or hunting for her keys in the morning,
which she does often, lose her keys
when she has to go to work, suggesting
she doesn't want to, and maybe this
is the problem with Jews:
they don't want to leave. Or they eat
lots of chicken. Or worry the black
of their skirts doesn't match the black
of their tops. Or like children more
than babies. Or fret over their mothers.
My Jewish problem is figuring out
why America in 2016 has a dab
of 1930s German Fascism to it—
people at political rallies
yelling crap about the Jews.
If I thought it would do any good,
I'd go to Topeka or wherever
and bring Eve with her troubled wardrobe
and her love of chicken and fascination
with children between two and thirteen,
when they can talk but before
they've begun planning the murder
of their parents, bring her face-to-face
with the screamers and ask, So these
are the freckles you hate? I would—we have
a lot of Amex points and I've never been
to Topeka or wherever, and I'm sure wherever
is very nice. And whenever we travel

to wherever, whatever people say
and however they say it, Eve's freckles
will be the same, kind of cute
and kind of Jewish,
just like all her other parts
that do and do not have freckles,
in an inventory I alone
get to take, though trust me—
after repeated inspection, I can attest
that underneath it all, she, like many
of the people you know or are,
is ticklish, wrinkly, sexy, scarred—
since Jews really are relentless
when it comes to being human.

## If the shoe fits

Lately I've been kicking the tires
of white supremacy. White supremacists
hold rallies, which include marching,
which is good for the heart. They have a knack
for getting their screaming on TV.
They have a simple, uncomplicated message,
and I long to be a simple, uncomplicated person.
The problem is I don't know what to be
supremely proud of. A white man
invented the lightbulb. A different white man
created the glow-in-the-dark yo-yo. Yet another
owns the New England Patriots.
What we're most famous for, though,
what we're absolutely the ne plus ultra
and Mona Lisa of, is melding capitalism
and slavery, the theft of land and bodies and lying
about the nature of the theft of land and bodies.
For instance: black people have thicker nerve casings
and so feel less pain. While there's a kind
of ingenuity to that lie, a justification
for sleeping well despite the whip on your bedpost,
mostly it's evil and not the kind of achievement
to make me slip on a foam "We're #1" hand.
What if white men became supremely good
at making up for our past? Returned Florida
to the Choctaw, the Creek, helped put a woman
in the Oval and not just to dust or dream
of comely drapes, updated forty acres and a mule
to forty acres and an F-150 pickup?
I'd have to tilt my head to recognize the world
and wear an Italian suit

to flatter my newfound self-respect.
Any day now. Yes sir. Any day now.

## The point of life

is to go out and put my arms
around a horse. While it might appear
from the road I'm cheating
on my wife, I'm cheating
on being sad that I'm a person
by holding the pulse of a horse
against my ear. I've also rested a cloud
against my ear at the top of a mountain,
and the bottom of a mountain
against my ear by lying down
and listening for the earth
grinding its teeth. I usually
bring a carrot I pulled up myself
from where it was hiding in the ground,
the horse always eats the carrot
I usually bring, this is certainly
almost certainty in a world famous
for making up its mind every second
who lives and dies, who looks good
in plaid or in the back of a squad car,
crying. The owner of the horse
doesn't know I've stolen her dew
on my pants or kissed her horse's neck
while wind stirs the shadows of grass,
I don't know if I flew as a boy
on the horse outside the grocery store
my mother always let me ride,
she'd put a coin in and go shop
and the horse would try hard
to run away and set both of us free:
when it couldn't, I'd settle
for finding my mother a little later

holding a can of something
trying to keep us alive.
I'd like the woman who owns the horse
and my mother, who'll always
have dibs on me, to meet.
While they talk, the horse and I
will continue our thought experiment:
if a man sees himself clearly
only in the brown mirror
of a horse's eyes, is he reborn
every time she blinks?

## Pacific

This kid had never seen the ocean,
I'd never seen a kid seeing the ocean
for the first time, and the ocean
had never been this close to Main Street,
according to the woman behind the desk
at the hotel, where the night before,
a moth landed on my shoulder, along with the moon.
He told us he was from up north,
then pointed at a man and woman fighting
so far away, we couldn't hear what they were saying
while their arms were furious with the air.
It's so big, he said.
The biggest thing in the world
that isn't the world, I thought
would be a way to put it, but just nodded.
By standing still next to his standing still
and my wife's, I was hoping
we'd build a little shelter for him,
a moment he could hold in the car
during the long drive with his untamed parents
and think, It was nice,
listening to the radio of the ocean
with those people.
But that's the kind of thought
I'd have in a poem, not what a kid would think
at all. And it was rude
to tell the moth it was a symbol of death.
It reminded me of snowflakes on my shoulder,
another kind of softness
that doesn't last, except as the desire
to carry someone barefoot over broken glass.

## Mirror

Woke to this on Google: another black man
cop-shot. He was already on the ground.
I didn't read why because there's always
a reason. He had a gun gun or a toy gun
or a hand that looked like it might have once
been or held a gun. He was on crack or PCP
or vitamins. He was too big, too powerful,
too feral for three cops, six cops, $x$ cops
to control. It was dark and he was dark.
It was sunny and he was dark. Every time
a cop kills a black man—whether the cop
is brown or black or white—the killing
is white. I am killing these men and want me
to stop. If you're listening to yourself
write this poem, know the world
knows who we are. I'll spread my hand
across your heart, our heart, so you'll feel
it's a friend asking, *How do you want to live?*
But please—don't keep looking like me
and saying this is justice. This is hunting.

## For love of the game

Early in the first quarter,
after an incomplete pass, we gathered
in the huddle and called Stephen Hawking
to ask, In an entropic system, what's the value
of ritualized violence? He thought
it was the huddle itself, that men pretended
for a moment a circle could hold them,
then tried to kill one another, then returned
to the circle, which is the moon, the womb,
a symbol of perfection as well as our desire
to achieve it. I tried to tell the cornerback
covering me how noble life is, but he thought
*A Brief History of Time* went on too long
and wasn't about to be distracted by my idea
that in failing to be perfect, we embody
the slight disruptions in DNA or alterations
in an environment that make evolution
possible. He felt every play
was a little version of the big bang,
an explosion into barely ordered disarray,
followed by collapse, and wished we'd go back
to talking about women or Greek mythology
as in the old days, when football
was football and men cried only
when shot or their dogs died
or they realized that war
was their most memorable achievement.
I was so moved by his wisdom
that I could have kissed this guy,
but face masks make that impossible.
Fear of the homoerotic is why the face mask
exists, Susan Sontag explained

to the Green Bay Packers
when they called her on fourth and one
not long before she died
and they couldn't decide what men
are more afraid of, death or love? She said
fear of death *is* fear of love,
and to go for it, you nancy boys.

## Hold your breath: a song of climate change

The water's rising
but we're not drowning yet.
When we're drowning
we'll do something.
When we're on our roofs.
When we're deciding between saving
the cute baby or the smart baby.
When there aren't enough helicopters
or news crews to circle
over everyone. When sharks
are in the streets. When people
are dying. When people
with wine cellars
are dying. We'll build dams
and dikes, put stilts
on our V-8s and golf courses,
cut down anyone
who cuts down a tree,
paint our Jesuses
green, we'll grow wings, we'll go
to the moon. Soon.

## Poof

At the party she said she wakes
every night 2:05ish and can't get back
to being gone, comes down and puts
five plates away, whatever's
in the dishwasher, has a frozen
or two daiquiris, takes a knife
and works at the hole in her head
until dawn and footsteps and lies
to hubby and kids she slept fine.
Too bad Sisyphus isn't here, I thought.
He'd move the rock in her heart
or at least offer insight
on being stuck. But while I
was thinking Greek, she noticed
all she'd said and turned pink.
Isn't it weird blushing
draws attention
instead of camouflaging the face
to fit in with the drapes? Pink
and looked down at her feet
doing nothing, so made them move
a little forward and back.
I did the same with mine
until I was tapping her shoe
and saying I miss when kickball
was a nutritious part of my day.
She remembered running
and sending a dragon on a kite
so high, it was scary to look at
far off and alone
or think of pulling home
and away from its new life

in the sky, so let it go.
I remembered that too
from the day before, the tumbling
feeling of reverse vertigo,
of doing something wrong
by trying to be free.
There's an intimacy
unique to the little tent
two people can put up at a party,
a species of speech as open
as it is never
to be spoken of again. I am almost
as no good today
as I was no good decades ago
at being human. The thing I like
about Sisyphus—he gets us.

## The impulse: to hold

This. This greenest green. Green of this forest,
this second, of electron transfer reactions
in thylakoid membranes. Green related to Old English
*grōwan,* to grow. Green of the heart chakra,
of leaves richer than money. I look up
from a hoe, a stove, from words I've read
so many times they've erased my eyes, look up
and know: every green after this green
is less so. Less sun-addled and sentient
and kind. Did you know hemoglobin
and chlorophyll have similar structures?
That we're almost trees
almost being us. O hyperemerald cousins.
O o. This minute, this fingersnap,
this wavelength of five hundred
and seventy nanometers. I look up
from my subatomic dismemberment
and feel summer's about to lose
its swashbuckle, its shine, become hangdog,
self-referential, blind.
Green of the tipping point
between the world being drinkable
and the world being dry. This instant
sheened by thriving. Doe-shy. Startled.
Gone as soon as I'm thrilled it's here.
This luck. This wish. This life.

## The roots of geometry

It was just a lump of fat
below my wife's nipple. Thank god
I didn't have to text people
the news of a scalpel. Not like B.
for H. "Out of surgery. Doing fine."
Not like C. for L. S. for S.
Add an O—SOS: save our sisters.
I have four of those. My mother
is the author of eight breasts.
None of my sisters
has the philosopher's taste
for martyrdom, the mechanic's taste
for oil, the aerialist's taste
for release from the dress of gravity.
But they all have bodies
and have entered the time of lessing:
anyone I touch
can touch the person next to them—
next in age, next in love—
and be only one further touch away
from a scar. What a weird
game of tag. I prefer
when a stream touches a river
touches a watershed touches an ocean,
not the one we came from
but so much like it, who cares
to split hairs. Just a glob of fat.
Still, I'm picturing cutting
and wincing. Picturing hands
handing over and over
pieces of my wife's life
that have been unlifed.

Is imagining an amulet
against happening? Do we repeat
what we fear until it's as small
and comforting as a baby's rattle
in our heads? A friend
feels her flesh not being there,
ghost breasts she wonders
if a ghost child suckles.
I picture the not-head
bent to the not-milk and still
turn away, build a tent
in my own thoughts for them both
of privacy. The first intimacy.
How did the circle
find us?
Mother and child.

## Getting there

Anas and I had Oreos this morning, as we do
once a week, on the bench outside his store,
sharing them so we don't get fat
(ter). Now and then, for a change,
Nutter Butters. Anas keeps a picture
of his mother above the register.
Right before he was shot three years ago
by a thief, he focused on her face.
Asked weeks later by a cop
what the man looked like, Anas thought
but didn't say, *Home.* He told me that.
I told my wife, who told her mother,
who told her mother, who said, How lovely.
Even in her senility, her eyes sparked
to the word *home.* Anas's wife is dead,
his mother, grandmother, but I've lent him
three generations of women
admiring his thoughts. Below
being a man, he's Anas. Beneath
being Syrian, he prefers Paris.
Under wanting to get even, he doesn't.
Retribution is like playing catch
with an egg. How far would we get with war
if every man first asked his mother,
Can I kill? Most of whom would say,
"It's *may* I kill, and no, you may not."

## Cleaning house

My cassettes are in a cardboard box
by the road. I don't remember
carrying them away. I must have taken Ambien
and done this in my sleep.
Sleepcleaning the garage
is more productive than sleepwalking,
unless it's sleepwalking to the bodega
for a pint of milk and a diamond.
No one will want the cassettes.
They're a defeated technology.
The war of ideas is brutal.
Typewriters can only get work now
as anchors for small boats. Trains
got beat up by cars. At least the spoon
is safe as long as soup exists.
But the cassettes serve
a spiritual purpose: they're a confession.
I'm old, they admit. I believe
in the singer-songwriter—
another defeated technology—they shout.
Also my actions, vis-à-vis the tapes,
pass the Turing test: I am not
a robot. As do my actions
vis-à-vis the melancholy habits
of dusk, the absence of actual wolves
in my heart, the bread-like aroma
of stars: I flail, dance backward,
I scream at trees for never once
putting an arm around me. These
are my Romantic actions and reactions.
My Romantic inactions outnumber them
by a country mile: the time I didn't

invent love, the time I didn't
solve the problem of human consciousness,
the time I never was born
a one-man band. When people
are a defeated technology,
who will leave us
where, what cherishing will occur
in regard to our hands and faces, our singing
about all the people we've loved
who didn't love us back? The broken heart,
as much as we've placed it
at the center of our cities
and flower arrangements, will be forgotten
when the wind is just the wind
and not a voice at the door
asking us to run away with it
and touch everything in the world
at least once a day, if not more.

# Poem that walks from fact to wish

I was a skinhead

in look and seem, a balding guy trying out the future
with a shaved head while wearing blue jeans and a white T
and grinding up one of Seattle's more Everesty hills,
when I was met by the real deal cruising the other way,

five shit-kickered dudes inked in swastikas
and Nazi daggers dripping blood, who nodded deep,
like dipping a bucket in a well, marking me as a brother
in hate, and passed before I could confess my lack of tats
and love of a Mexican Jew, I mean a kikey spic, I mean
there's never time to get scientific and mushy
on guys trying to act the part of death,
to do what all good parents teach their tots to do
when meeting lives this unmoored, this lost at sea—
you whip out the statistical work of Joseph Chang:

"Our findings suggest a remarkable proposition:
no matter the languages we speak or the color
of our skin, we share ancestors who planted rice
on the banks of the Yangtze, who first domesticated horses
on the steppes of the Ukraine, who hunted giant sloths
in the forests of North and South America,
and who labored to build the Great Pyramid of Khufu."

I promised myself that next time I'd be Johnny-on-the-spot
with the intellectual nunchucks, that I'd ease their longing
for a homeland by telling them we've all got a home
in Africa, where every soul currently huffing and puffing
got its ancient start, and that white isn't a race,
a cutting apart, so much as an adaptation,

the process of learning to get along
with snow, *I would I would I would I would I would I would*

I brainchanted to myself while powering up the hill
and channeling the French, who so hiply invented éclairs,
and Paris, and esprit de l'escalier, or staircase wit,
when the right thing to say zooms to mind
as you're walking away and have time to edit the past
to redress your failure to be brilliant, or in this case,
as in most cases, kind.

## There it is

My parents will be dead soon.
I'm going to call today and ask for advice
or a loan I don't need to make them feel
they're still important cogs in the machine
of whatever this is. Even though
they won't remember the call
during the call, or the sun or me
or sock puppets when they're dead.
I say that, but the dead could have
an abiding fondness for sock puppets,
or float around the heads of their children
as a kind of dust that makes everyone sneeze.
Though I don't actually want persistence
to be true, the soul to be true. I want
some kind of going home for them, going back
to whatever made the universe happen
in the first place, and that the living
have to cry sorting through the photos
and Crescent wrenches left behind
and feel the teeth of solitude
when their parents are dead, just like any star
light-years from any other star
or a rock in a field waiting and waiting
for the hand that will never come along
and give it a fling. I want pain. Nights of wondering
what the point of life is and mornings
of stretching not enough coffee
into two cups and feeling a little better
opening a window to listen
to the traffic jam of birds. I've asked people
and dogs and bears and the moon
in all its phases what the soul is,

filled notebooks with my inability to draw
a conclusion or a face that doesn't look
like Silly String taking a shit, built go-karts
and boxes and sheds and a beautiful bathroom
without letting on to anyone
that each is a temple where I pray
for greater understanding
of why we need to understand,
and bears in particular were very clear on this—
the soul is people missing you
when you're gone, no more, no less
than a bond persisting
through the impossibility of the bond. One day soon
I'll look at the ass and back shapes of my parents
sitting together for years watching TV
and want to carry their chairs in my arms
and blood everywhere I go, molds of their bodies
the nearest thing to the real deal,
which is exactly the stupid wishing
that things were different
the bears said makes up the soul,
and urged me to indulge
as if devouring a tree of mulberries
with no thought to whether next year
there'd be more.

## Going the extra mile in leaving no stone unturned

The sequence—one strum of a banjo,
one shot fired at a steel chicken,
thirty seconds of crying, ten seconds
of lightly tapping my skull
with a ball-peen hammer—all repeated—
all recorded and e-mailed to a listserv
of women as obsessed with the movie *Aliens*
as I am—in the belief
that I've tried humming "Over the Rainbow"
in Notre-Dame; rowing a boat;
doing coke and speed; feeling special
whenever I've seen a bear;
loving Rickie Lee Jones's *Pirates;*
eating a peanut butter and jelly rice cake
for breakfast; adoring the smell
of my wife's vagina; honesty;
employing a strict "No fireflies
will be harmed on my watch" policy;
mistaking rivers for garage bands;
looking on the backsides of paintings,
mirrors, lightning for the truth;
drunk-dialing my younger self;
sober-dialing my CAT scan results;
telling crickets to shut up;
telling crickets to turn it up;
and still I have a wrong turn
for a heart—and if god

or absence asks, About that trouble
you had being alive, did you try
one strum of a banjo,
one shot fired at a steel chicken,

thirty seconds of crying, ten seconds
of lightly tapping your skull
with a ball-peen hammer—all repeated—
all recorded and e-mailed to a listserv
of women as obsessed with the movie *Aliens*
as you were—and I can't honestly say Yes
to god or absence, Yes, I did try that—
if I haven't tried everything I can possibly try—
I won't deserve the example of Ripley—
terrified but stepping forward
into the terror—kicking its ass
but not really—kicking its ass
but only for a while—what else
is there—chocolate,
I know—chocolate
and this other thing—you know
what it is—so why
won't you tell me?

## Lights on, lights off

I know I couldn't pet our cat's paws
when she was young, but can now
after thirteen years together. I know wood smoke
makes the air smell warmer. I know I become elated
ten minutes after a first drink, melancholy
half an hour after a second. I know I've wasted
most of my life on consciousness, on counting
and tic-tac-toe. I know if you're going to stare
at a prostitute in a window in Amsterdam,
you should be naked, too. And yes,
I know the sword of Damocles
is stuck in my head. And no,
I don't know how it got there,
when the thread of happiness broke. And yes,
it has complicated my relationship
with hats. And no, it doesn't hurt
except when I stand on my head.
I like that we share
these epistemological interludes.
Now, though, I want to return to the dark,
to waiting for morning to touch everything
in this room and bring it all back to life
simultaneously, a resurrection
only the sun is capable of, having more fingers
than all the people now
or ever alive. And yet, despite this intimacy,
what do I really know about the sun,
I mean personally?

## My most recent position paper

A little bit of hammering
goes a long way toward making
the kind of noise I want my heart
to look up to—or have you ever
gone into a woods and applauded the light
that fights its way to the ground,
and the shadows, and the explosions
of feathers where blue jays
have been ripped into the bright
and hungry future of hawks—
and there's this—writing an étude
by pushing pianos off a cliff
until one of them howls or whispers
just so—like a vagrant
slipping into a clean bed
or a man lifting a dying child
toward the sun and begging help,
rescue—if my eyes could speak,
they'd be mouths—the tongues
of my fingers ask to be words
against your skin—and when I
was a librarian, I lost my job
for exhorting patrons to sing
"Bye, bye, Miss American Pie"—
it's not what we do here, I was told—
yet I know this is a world
made by volcanoes, and don't want
to keep this awareness of kaboom
to myself—so have picked up
my zither and begun walking
and strumming like an idiot
who thinks music is all

a body needs to feed itself—
and though I haven't eaten
in years, I have been fed.

## Home improvement in memoriam

Two poets died this past month
I knew in person a little and a lot
by what they wrote about forests and saints.
Their deaths got me over the hump
of swapping out the hollow plastic doors
in my house for solid oak, which I wanted to do
for years but only now does the genuine
shine as worth whatever trouble it takes
to match the old hinge locations to the new doors.
I've done one, and for days as I glide
through the house, I'm pulled to the bedroom
to touch the revelations of the grain,
or I'll be out counting falling leaves
for the annual inventory or riding on a deer
across the field when I think of the door
and become convinced that someone—not me—
will live forever or at least
have their growth penciled onto that door jamb
and come back before they die to kiss
the stages of reaching their life went through,
long after I'm gone and no one knows
all the places I've buried dead cats
around this yard, not just because I love animals
and digging holes, but those are two reasons
to do a lot of things: feed the birds
and elephants if ever they arrive, and move dirt
from one hiding place to another,
to honor the spirit of the unsettled earth.

# The class visit

How many of you have seen a hawk?
One hand raised. Who's gone
to Disney World? No hands raised.
How many of you own a dog? Four hands.
Has anyone ever made a snowman? Two hands.
Ever seen the Big Dipper?
On my grandma's farm, one kid said,
his hand up, fingers wiggling.
Who knows someone who was shot
and killed? Every hand went up. Faster
than thought. More certain than rain.
If you know someone else
who was killed, raise your other hand.
Had you happened by just then,
you'd wonder why so many kids
were signaling touchdown, both arms
thrown high, or why that class
was pretending to be on a roller coaster,
arms tossed at the sun
as they dropped over the edge
of their fake demise,
and smile. An actual smile
or just a bit of joy
you'd carry on your face
down the hall,
to wherever you were going,
making the mood
of the next room you entered
a little better,
even if you didn't know it.
I think the pleasure
has to do with their hands

being so little
yet wanting to hold as much
as anyone has ever wanted to hold.
Hands are good at that. Holding.
Hands are good at almost everything
we ask them to do.

## Acknowledgments

Poems in *Hold* first appeared in the Academy of American Poets Poem-a-Day, *The Adroit Journal, AGNI, The American Journal of Poetry, The American Poetry Review, Catamaran, Conduit, Diode, FIELD, The Gettysburg Review, Green Mountains Review, Grist, Guernica, The Journal, Kenyon Review, The Massachusetts Review, Narrative, New England Review, New World Writing, The North, The Paris-American, Pleiades, Poetry Northwest, Rattle, Rise Up Review, Smartish Pace, The Southern Review,* and the anthology *Resistance, Rebellion, Life: 50 Poems Now.*

## About the Author

*Hold* is Bob Hicok's ninth collection. His seventh, *Elegy Owed*, was a finalist for the National Book Critics Circle Award. *This Clumsy Living* was awarded the 2008 Bobbitt Prize from the Library of Congress; Luxbooks published a German translation in 2013. *Animal Soul* was a finalist for the 2001 National Book Critics Circle Award. *The Legend of Light* received the Felix Pollak Prize in Poetry and was named an ALA Notable Book of 1997. Hicok is the recipient of eight Pushcart prizes, a Guggenheim, and two NEA fellowships. His poetry has been selected for inclusion in nine volumes of *Best American Poetry*. He teaches at Virginia Tech.

Poetry is vital to language and living. Since 1972, Copper Canyon Press has published extraordinary poetry from around the world to engage the imaginations and intellects of readers, writers, booksellers, librarians, teachers, students, and donors.

**WE ARE GRATEFUL FOR THE MAJOR SUPPORT PROVIDED BY:**

THE PAUL G. ALLEN
FAMILY FOUNDATION

 amazon *literary partnership*

 the point
envision · enact · evolve

 **4
CULTURE**

 golden lasso

 **Lannan**

 ART WORKS. | National Endowment for the Arts
arts.gov

 **A&**
OFFICE OF ARTS & CULTURE
SEATTLE

 WASHINGTON STATE
ARTS COMMISSION

TO LEARN MORE ABOUT UNDERWRITING
COPPER CANYON PRESS TITLES,
PLEASE CALL 360-385-4925 EXT. 103

**WE ARE GRATEFUL FOR THE MAJOR SUPPORT PROVIDED BY:**

Anonymous

Jill Baker and Jeffrey Bishop

Anne and Geoff Barker

Donna and Matt Bellew

John Branch

Diana Broze

Sarah and Tim Cavanaugh

Beatrice R. and Joseph A. Coleman
    Foundation

Laurie and Oskar Eustis

Mimi Gardner Gates

Linda Gerrard and Walter Parsons

Nancy Gifford

Gull Industries Inc. on behalf of
    Ruth and William True

The Trust of Warren A. Gummow

Phil Kovacevich and Eric Wechsler

Lakeside Industries Inc. on behalf
    of Jeanne Marie Lee

Maureen Lee and Mark Busto

Rhoady Lee and Alan Gartenhaus

Ellie Mathews and Carl Youngmann
    as The North Press

Anne O'Donnell and John Phillips

Petunia Charitable Fund and
    adviser Elizabeth Hebert

Gay Phinney

Suzie Rapp and Mark Hamilton

Emily and Dan Raymond

Jill and Bill Ruckelshaus

Kim and Jeff Seely

Richard Swank

University Research Council of
    DePaul University

Vincentian Endowment Foundation

Dan Waggoner

Barbara and Charles Wright

Caleb Young and Keep It Cinematic

The dedicated interns and
    faithful volunteers of
    Copper Canyon Press

The Chinese character for poetry is made up of two parts:
"word" and "temple." It also serves as pressmark for
Copper Canyon Press.

The poems are set in Janson. The display type is
Berthold Akzidenz-Grotesk Condensed.
Book design and composition by Phil Kovacevich.